God
Always
Cares

C H Spurgeon

Christian Focus Publications Ltd.

Published by
Christian Focus Publications Ltd
Geanies House
Fearn, Tain
Ross-shire IV20 1TW
Scotland

© 1990 Christian Focus Publications Ltd.
ISBN 1 871676 39 8

CONTENTS

Page

Preface

What believer does not warm to the words of the 23rd Psalm? Probably the best-known psalm in the world, Spurgeon leads the reader unerringly into a deeper and clearer understanding of its great comfort.

The music of Psalm 46 has been ringing in my ears from boyhood days. I don't mean the tune we sang, but the majesty and calm-inducing power of the words themselves. And who better than Spurgeon to open up their meaning and challenge the reader to "make sure each one of you of your portion in God," i.e. make sure you have been reconciled to him?

After the Lord graciously drew me to himself as a sinner

needing his free forgiveness in my teens, it was often my delight to sing in our parish church what was introduced as the Jubilate Deo, Psalm 100. I wish I had seen Spurgeon's pithy and helpful comments earlier!

Psalm 46 makes good reading for those going through any time of trouble, while the words of Psalm 100 can just as helpfully lead the thoughts and praises of those who experienced God's deliverances in the last decade of the twentieth century as surely as they ever did in Spurgeon's day.

What Christian family has not read Psalm 121 over the breakfast table before a loved member of that family set out on a long or difficult journey, or moved into a new phase of life? Maybe we read it with a lump in our throat! Spurgeon leads us into a deeper understanding of this wonderful psalm. What firm footing for our steps in our onward pilgrimage to heaven, the City that has foundations more firm than anything in this fallen world.

"Keep your eyes upon Jesus
Let nobody else take his place,
So that hour by hour
You may prove his power,
Till at last you have won the great race."

I recommend this volume to the reader.

Leith Samuel
Southampton

Psalm 46

GOD *is* our refuge and strength, a very present help in trouble.

2 Therefore will not we fear, though the earth be removed, and though the mountains be carried into the midst of the sea;

3 *Though* the waters thereof roar *and* be troubled, *though* the mountains shake with the swelling thereof. Selah.

4 *There is* a river, the streams whereof shall make glad the city of God, the holy *place* of the tabernacles of the Most High.

5 God *is* in the midst of her; she shall not be moved: God shall help her, *and that* right

early.

6 The heathen raged, the kingdoms were moved: he uttered his voice, the earth melted.

7 The LORD of hosts is with us; the God of Jacob *is* our refuge. Selah.

8 Come, behold the works of the LORD, what desolations he hath made in the earth.

9 He maketh wars to cease unto the end of the earth; he breaketh the bow, and cutteth the spear in sunder; he burneth the chariot in the fire.

10 Be still, and know that I *am* God: I will be exalted among the heathen, I will be exalted in the earth.

11 The LORD of hosts *is* with us; the God of Jacob *is* our refuge. Selah.

1. *"God is our refuge and strength."* Not our armies, or our fortresses. Israel's boast is in Jehovah, the only living and true God. Others vaunt their impregnable castles, placed on inaccessible rocks, and secured with gates of iron, but God is a far better refuge from distress than all these: and when the time comes to carry the war into the enemy's territories, the Lord stands his people in better stead than all the valour of legions or the boasted strength of chariot and horse. Soldiers of the cross, remember this, and count yourselves safe, and make yourselves strong in God. Forget not the personal posses-

sive word *"our;"* make sure, each one, of your portion in God, that you may say, "He is *my* refuge and strength." Neither forget the fact that God is our refuge just now, in the immediate present, as truly as when David penned the word. God alone is our all in all. All other refuges are refuges of lies, all other strength is weakness, for power belongeth unto God: but as God is all-sufficient, our defence and might are equal to all emergencies.

"A very present help in trouble," or *in distresses he has so been found*, he has been tried and proved by his people. He never withdraws himself from his afflicted. He is their help, truly, effectually, constantly;

he is present or near them, close at their side and ready for their succour, and this is emphasized by the word "*every*" in our version, he is more present than friend or relative can be, yea, more nearly present than even the trouble itself. To all this comfortable truth is added the consideration that his assistance comes at the needed time. He is not as the swallows that leave us in the winter; he is a friend in need and a friend indeed. When it is very dark with us, let brave spirits say, "Come, let us sing the forty-sixth Psalm".

"A fortress firm, and steadfast rock,
    Is God in time of danger;
A shield and sword in every shock,
    From foe well-known or stranger".

2. "*Therefore*." How fond

the psalmist is of therefores! his poetry is no poetic rapture without reason, it is as logical as a mathematical demonstration. The next words are a necessary inference from these. "Will not we fear." With God on our side, how irrational would fear be! Where he is all power is, and all love, why therefore should we quail? *Though the earth be removed*," though the basis of all visible things should be so convulsed as to be entirely changed. "*And though the mountains be carried into the midst of the sea;*" though the firmest of created objects should fall to headlong ruin, and be submerged in utter destruction. The two phrases set forth the most terrible commotions within the range of imagination, and include the overthrow of dynasties, the destruction of nations, the ruin of families, the persecutions of the church, the reign of heresy, and whatever else may at any time try the faith of believers. Let the worst come to the worst, the child of God should never give way to mistrust; since God remaineth faithful there can be no danger to his cause or people. When the elements shall melt with fervent heat, and the heavens and the earth shall pass away in the last general conflagration, we shall serenely behold "the wreck of matter, and the crash of worlds," for even then our refuge shall preserve us from all evil, our strength shall prepare us for all good.

3. *"Though the waters there-of roar and be troubled."* When all things are excited to fury, and reveal their utmost power to disturb, faith smiles serenely. She is not afraid of noise, nor even of real force, she knows that the Lord stilleth the raging of the sea, and holdeth the waves in the hollow of his hand. *"Though the mountains shake with the swelling thereof."* Alps and Andes may tremble, but faith rests on a firmer basis, and is not to be moved by swelling seas. Evil may ferment, wrath may boil, and pride may foam, but the brave heart of holy confidence trembles not. Great men who are like mountains may quake for fear in times of great calamity, but the man whose trust is in

God needs never be dismayed.

"*Selah*." In the midst of such a hurly-burly the music may well come to a pause, both to give the singers breath, and ourselves time for meditation. We are in no hurry, but can sit us down and wait while earth dissolves, and mountains rock, and oceans roar. Ours is not the headlong rashness which passes for courage, we can calmly confront the danger, and meditate upon terror, dwelling on its separate items and united forces. The pause is not an exclamation of dismay, but merely a rest in music; we do not suspend our song in alarm, but retune our harps with deliberation amidst the tumult of the storm. It were well if all of us could say, "*Selah*," under tempestuous trials, but alas! too often we speak in our haste, lay our trembling hands bewildered among the strings, strike the lyre with a rude crash, and mar the melody of our life-song.

4. *There is a river*. Divine grace like a smoothly flowing, fertilising, full, and never-failing river, yields refreshment and consolation to believers. This is the river of the water of life, of which the church above as well as the church below partakes evermore. It is no boisterous ocean, but a placid stream, it is not stayed in its course by earthquakes or crumbling mountains, it follows its serene course without disturbance. Happy are they who know from their own experi-

ence that there is such a river of God.

"*The streams whereof*" in their various influences, for they are many, "*shall make glad the city of God*," by assuring the citizens that Zion's Lord will unfailingly supply all their needs. The streams are not transient like Cherith, nor muddy like the Nile, nor furious like Kishon, nor treacherous like Job's deceitful brooks, neither are their waters "naught" like those of Jericho, they are clear, cool, fresh, abundant, and gladdening. The great fear of an Eastern city in time of war was lest the water supply should be cut off during a seige; if that were secured the city could hold out against attacks for an indefinite period.

In this verse, Jerusalem, which represents the church of God, is described as well supplied with water, to set forth the fact, that in seasons of trial all-sufficient grace will be given to enable us to endure unto the end. The church is like a well-ordered city, surrounded with mighty walls of truth and justice, garrisoned by omnipotence, fairly built and adorned by infinite wisdom: its burgesses the saints enjoy high privileges; they trade with far-off lands, they live in the smile of the King; and as a great river is the very making and mainstay of a town, so is the broad river of everlasting love and grace their joy and bliss. The church is peculiarly the "*City of God*," of his designing, building, election, purchasing and indwelling. It is dedicated to his praise, and glorified by his presence.

"The holy place of the tabernacles of the Most High." This was the peculiar glory of Jerusalem, that the Lord within her walls had a place where he peculiarly revealed himself, and this is the choice privilege of the saints, concerning which we may cry with wonder, "Lord, how is it that thou wilt manifest thyself unto us, and not unto the world?" To be a temple for the Holy Ghost is the delightful portion of each saint, to be the living temple for the Lord our God is also the high honour of the church in her corporate capacity. Our God is here called by a worthy title, indicating his power,

majesty, sublimity, and excellency; and it is worthy of note that under this character he dwells in the church. We have not a great God in nature, and a little God in grace; no, the church contains as clear and convincing a revelation of God as the works of nature, and even more amazing in the excellent glory which shines between the cherubim overshadowing that mercy seat which is the centre and gathering place of the people of the living God. To have the Most High dwelling within her members, is to make the church on earth like the church in heaven.

5. *"God is in the midst of her."* His help is therefore sure and near. Is she besieged, then he is himself besieged within

her, and we may be certain that he will break forth upon his adversaries. How near is the Lord to the distresses of his saints, since he sojourns in their midst! Let us take heed that we do not grieve him; let us have such respect to him as Moses had when he felt the sand of Horeb's desert to be holy, and put off his shoes from off his feet when the Lord spake from the burning bush.

"She shall not be moved." How can she be moved unless her enemies move her Lord also? His presence renders all hope of capturing and de-molishing the city utterly ridi-culous. The Lord is in the vessel, and she cannot, there-fore, be wrecked. *"God shall help her."* Within her he will

furnish rich supplies, and outside her walls he will lay her foes in heaps like the armies of Sennacherib, when the angel went forth and smote them.

"And that right early." As soon as the first ray of light proclaims the coming day, at the turning of the morning God's right arm shall be outstretched for his people. The Lord is up betimes. We are slow to meet him, but he is never tardy in helping us. Impatience complains of divine delays, but in very deed the Lord is not slack concerning his promise. Man's haste is often folly, but God's apparent delays are ever wise; and, when rightly viewed, are no delays at all. To-day the bands of evil may environ the church of God, and threaten

her with destruction; but ere
long they shall pass away like
the foam on the waters, and the
noise of their tumult shall be
silent in the grave. The darkest
hour of the night is just before
the turning of the morning; and
then, even then, shall the Lord
appear as the great ally of his
church.

6. *"The heathen raged."* The
nations were in a furious up-
roar, they gathered against the
city of the Lord like wolves
ravenous for their prey; they
foamed, and roared, and swel-
led like a tempestuous sea.
"The kingdoms were moved."
A general confusion seized upon society; the fierce invaders
convulsed their own dominions
by draining the population to
urge on the war, and they

desolated other territories by their devastating march to Jerusalem. Crowns fell from royal heads, ancient thrones rocked like trees driven of the tempest, powerful empires fell like pines uprooted by the blast; everything was in disorder, and dismay seized on all who knew not the Lord.

"He uttered his voice, the earth melted." With no other instrumentality than a word the Lord ruled the storm. He gave forth a voice and stout hearts were dissolved, proud armies were annihilated, conquering powers were enfeebled. At first the confusion appeared to be worse confounded, when the element of divine power came into view; the very earth seemed turned to wax, the most

24

solid and substantial of human things melted like the fat of rams upon the altar; but anon peace followed, the rage of man subsided, hearts capable of repentance relented, and the implacable were silenced. How mighty is a word from God! How mighty the Incarnate Word. O that such a word would come from the excellent glory even now to melt all hearts in love to Jesus, and to end for ever all the persecutions, wars, and rebellions of men!

7. *"The Lord of hosts is with us."* This is the reason for all Zion's security, and for the overthrow of her foes. The Lord rules the angels, the stars, the elements, and all the hosts of heaven; and the heaven of

heavens are under his sway. The armies of men though they know it not are made to subserve his will. This General of the forces of the land, and the Lord High Admiral of the seas, is on our side — our august ally; woe unto those who fight against him, for they shall fly like smoke before the wind when he gives the word to scatter them. *"The God of Jacob is our refuge."* Immanuel is Jehovah of Hosts, and Jacob's God is our high place of defence. When this glad verse is sung to music worthy of such a jubilate, well may the singers pause and the players wait awhile to retune their instruments; here, therefore, fitly stands that solemn, stately, peaceful note of rest. SELAH.

8. *"Come, behold the works of the Lord."* The joyful citizens of Jerusalem are invited to go forth and view the remains of their enemies, that they may mark the prowess of Jehovah and the spoil which his right hand hath won for his people. It were well if we also carefully noted the providential dealings of our covenant God, and were quick to perceive his hand in the battles of his church. Whenever we read history it should be with this verse sounding in our ears. We should read the newspaper in the same spirit, to see how the Head of the Church rules the nations for his people's good, as Joseph governed Egypt for the sake of Israel. *What desolations he hath made in the earth."* The destroyers he

destroys, the desolators he desolates. How forcible is the verse at this date! The ruined cities of Assyria, Babylon, Petra, Bashan, Canaan, are our instructors, and in tables of stone record the doings of the Lord. In every place where his cause and crown have been disregarded ruin has surely followed: sin has been a blight on nations, and left their palaces to lie in heaps. In the days of the writer of this Psalm, there had probably occurred some memorable interposition of God against his Israel's foes; and as he saw their overthrow, he called on his fellow citizens to come forth and attentively consider the terrible things in righteousness which had been wrought on their behalf. Dismantled castles and ruined abbeys in our own land stand as memorials of the Lord's victories over oppression and superstition. May there soon be more of such desolations.

"Ye gloomy piles, ye tombs of living men,
Ye sepulchres of womanhood, or worse;
    Ye refuges of lies, soon may ye fall,
And 'mid your ruins may the owl, and bat,
And dragon find congenial resting place."

9. *"He maketh wars to cease unto the end of the earth."* His voice quiets the tumult of war, and calls for the silence of peace. However remote and barbarous the tribe, he awes the people into rest. He crushes the great powers till they cannot provoke strife again; he gives his people profound repose. *"He breaketh the bow,"* the sender of swift-winged

death he renders useless. "*And cutteth the spear in sunder*"— the lance of the mighty man he shivers. "*He burneth the chariot in the fire*"—the proud war-chariot with its death-dealing scythes he commits to the flames. All sorts of weapons he piles heaps on heaps, and utterly destroys them. So was it in Judea in the days of yore, so shall it be in all lands in eras yet to come. Blessed deed of the Prince of Peace! when shall it be literally performed? Already the spiritual foes of his people are despoiled of their power to destroy; but when shall the universal victory of peace be celebrated, and instruments of wholesale murder be consigned to ignominious destruction? How glorious will the ultimate victory of Jesus be in the day of his appearing, when every enemy shall lick the dust!

10. *"Be still, and know that I am God."* Hold off your hands, ye enemies! Sit down and wait in patience, ye believers! Acknowledge that Jehovah is God, ye who feel the terrors of his wrath! Adore him, and him only, ye who partake in the protections of his grace. Since none can worthily proclaim his nature, let "expressive silence muse his praise." The boasts of the ungodly and the timorous forebodings of the saints should certainly be hushed by a sight of what the Lord has done in past ages.

"I will be exalted among the heathen." They forget God,

they worship idols, but Jehovah will yet be honoured by them. Reader, the prospect of missions are bright, bright as the promises of God. Let no man's heart fail him; the solemn declarations of this verse must be fulfilled. *"I will be exalted in the earth,"* among all people, whatever may have been their wickedness or their degradation. Either by terror or love God will subdue all hearts to himself. The whole round earth shall yet reflect the light of his majesty. All the more because of the sin, and obstinacy, and pride of man shall God be glorified when grace reigns unto eternal life in all corners of the world.

11. *"The Lord of hosts is with us; the God of Jacob is our*

refuge." It was meet to sing this twice over. It is a truth of which no believer wearies, it is a fact too often forgotten, it is a precious privilege which cannot be too often considered. Reader, is the Lord on thy side? Is Emmanuel, God with us, thy Redeemer? Is there a covenant between thee and God as between God and Jacob? If so, thrice happy art thou. Show thy joy in holy song, and in times of trouble play the man by still making music for thy God.

SELAH. Here as before, lift up the heart. Rest in contemplation after praise. Still keep the soul in tune. It is easier to sing a hymn of praise than to continue in the spirit of praise, but let it be our aim to maintain the uprising devotion of our grateful hearts, and so end our song as if we intended it to be continued.

SELAH bids the music rest,
Pause in silence soft and blest;
SELAH bids uplift the strain,
Harps and voices tune again;
SELAH ends the vocal praise,
Still your hearts to God upraise.

Psalm 100

MAKE a joyful noise unto the LORD, all ye lands.

2 Serve the LORD with gladness: come before his presence with singing.

3 Know ye that the LORD he *is* God: *it is* he *that* hath made us and not we ourselves; *we are* his people, and the sheep of his pasture.

4 Enter into his gates with thanksgiving, *and* into his courts with praise: be thankful unto him, *and* bless his name.

5 For the LORD *is* good; his mercy *is* everlasting; and his truth *endureth* to all generations.

1. *"Make a joyful noise unto the* LORD, *all ye lands."* This is a repetition of the fourth verse of Psalm 98. The original word signifies a glad shout, such as loyal subjects give when their king appears among them. Our happy God should be worshipped by a happy people; a cheerful spirit is in keeping with his nature, his acts, and the gratitude which we should cherish for his mercies. In every land Jehovah's goodness is seen, therefore in every land should he be praised. Never will the world be in its proper condition till with one unanimous shout it adores the only God. O ye nations, how long

will ye blindly reject him? Your
golden age will never arrive till
ye with all your hearts revere
him.

2. "*Serve the* LORD *with gladness.*" "Glad homage pay with
awful mirth." He is our Lord,
and therefore he is to be served;
he is our gracious Lord, and
therefore to be served with joy.
The invitation to worship here
given is not a melancholy one,
as though adoration were a
funeral solemnity, but a cheery
gladsome exhortation, as
though we were bidden to a
marriage feast.

"*Come before his presence
with singing.*" We ought in
worship to realise the presence
of God, and by an effort of the
mind to approach him. This is
an act which must to every

rightly instructed heart be one of great solemnity, but at the same time it must not be performed in the servility of fear, and therefore we come before him, not with weepings and wailings, but with psalms and hymns. Singing, as it is a joyful, and at the same time a devout, exercise, should be a constant form of approach to God. The measured, harmonious, hearty utterance of praise by a congregation of really devout persons is not merely decorous but delightful, and is a fit anticipation of the worship of heaven, where praise has absorbed prayer, and become the sole mode of adoration. How a certain society of brethren can find it in their hearts to forbid singing in public worship is a riddle which we cannot solve. We feel inclined to say with Dr. Watts—

"Let those refuse to sing
Who never knew our God;
But favourites of the heavenly king
Must speak his praise abroad."

3. "*Know that the* LORD *he is God.*"Our worship must be intelligent. We ought to know whom we worship and why. "Man, know thyself," is a wise aphorism, yet to know our God is truer wisdom; and it is very questionable whether a man can know himself until he knows his God. Jehovah is God in the fullest, most absolute, and most exclusive sense: he is God alone; to know him in that character and prove our knowledge by obedience, trust, submission, zeal, and love is an

attainment which only grace can bestow. Only those who practically recognise his Godhead are at all likely to offer acceptable praise.

"It is he that hath made us, and not we ourselves." Shall not the creature reverence its maker? Some men live as if they made themselves; they call themselves "self-made men," and they adore their supposed creators; but Christians recognise the origin of their being and their well-being, and take no honour to themselves either for being, or for being what they are. Neither in our first or second creation dare we put so much as a finger upon the glory, for it is the sole right and property of the Almighty. To disclaim honour for ourselves is

as necessary a part of true reverence as to ascribe glory to the Lord. "Non nobis, domine!" will for ever remain the true believer's confession. Of late philosophy has laboured hard to prove that all things have been developed from atoms, or have, in other words, made themselves: if this theory shall ever find believers, there will certainly remain no reason for accusing the superstitious of credulity, for the amount of credence necessary to accept this dogma of scepticism is a thousandfold greater than that which is required even by an absurd belief in winking Madonnas, and smiling Bambinos. For our part, we find it far more easy to believe that the Lord made us than that we were developed by a long chain of natural selections from floating atoms which fashioned themselves.

"We are his people, and the sheep of his pasture." It is our honour to have been chosen from all the world besides to be *his* own people, and our privilege to be therefore guided by his wisdom, tended by his care, and fed by his bounty. Sheep gather around their shepherd and look up to him; in the same manner let us gather around the great Shepherd of mankind. The avowal of our relation to God is in itself praise; when we recount his goodness we are rendering to him the best adoration; our songs require none of the inventions of fictions, the bare facts are enough; the

simple narration of the mercies of the Lord is more astonishing that the productions of imagination. That we are the sheep of his pasture is a plain truth, and at the same time the very essence of poetry.

4. *"Enter into his gates with thanksgiving."* To the occurrence of the word *thanksgiving* in this place the psalm probably owes its title. In all our public service the rendering of thanks must abound; it is like the incense of the temple, which filled the whole house with smoke. Expiatory sacrifices are ended, but those of gratitude will never be out of date. So long as we are receivers of mercy we must be givers of thanks. Mercy permits us to enter his gates; let us praise that

mercy. What better subject for our thoughts in God's own house than the Lord of the house.

"*And into his courts with praise.*" Into whatever court of the Lord you may enter, let your admission be the subject of praise: thanks be to God, the innermost court is now open to believers, and we enter into that which is within the veil; it is incumbent upon us that we acknowledge the high privilege by our songs.

"*Be thankful unto him.*" Let the praise be in your heart as well as on your tongue, and let it all be for him to whom it all belongs. "*And bless his name.*" He blessed you, bless him in return; bless his name, his character, his person. What-

44

ever he does, be sure that you bless him for it; bless him when he takes away as well as when he gives; bless him as long as you live, under all circumstances; bless him in all his attributes, from whatever point of view you consider him.

5. "*For the* LORD *is good.*" This sums up his character and contains a mass of reasons for praise. He is good, gracious, kind, bountiful, loving; yea, God is love. He who does not praise the good is not good himself. The kind of praise inculcated in the psalm, viz., that of joy and gladness, is most fitly urged upon us by an argument from the goodness of God.

"*His mercy is everlasting.*" God is not mere justice, stern

45

and cold; he has bowels of compassion, and wills not the sinner's death. Towards his own people mercy is still more conspicuously displayed; it has been theirs from all eternity, and shall be theirs world without end. Everlasting mercy is a glorious theme for sacred song.

"And his truth endureth to all generations." No fickle being is he, promising and forgetting. He has entered into covenant with his people, and will never revoke it, nor alter the thing that has gone out of his lips. As our fathers found him faithful, so will our sons, and their seed for ever. A changeable God would be a terror to the righteous, they would have no sure anchorage, and amid a changing world they would be driven

to and fro in perpetual fear of shipwreck. It were well if the truth of divine faithfulness were more fully remembered by some theologians; it would overturn their belief in the final fall of believers, and teach them a more consolatory system. Our heart leaps for joy as we bow before One who has never broken his word or changed his purpose.

> "As well might he his being quit
> As break his promise or forget."

Resting on his sure word, we feel that joy which is here commanded, and in the strength of it we come into his presence even now, and speak good of his name.

Psalm 23

The LORD *is* my shepherd; I shall not want.

2 He maketh me to lie down in green pastures: he leadeth be beside the still waters.

3 He restoreth my soul: he leadeth me in the paths of righteousness for his name's sake.

4 Yea, though I walk through the valley of the sha- dow of death, I will fear no evil: for thou *art* with me; thy rod and thy staff they comfort me.

5 Thou preparest a table be- fore me in the presence of mine enemies: thou anointest my head with oil; my cup runneth

over.

6 Surely goodness and mercy shall follow me all the days of my life: and I will dwell in the house of the LORD for ever.

1. *"The Lord is my shepherd."* What condescension is this, that the Infinite Lord assumes towards his people the office and character of a Shepherd! It should be the subject of grateful admiration that the great God allows himself to be compared to anything which will set forth his great love and care for his own people. David had himself been a keeper of sheep, and understood both the needs of the sheep and the many cares of a shepherd. He compares himself to a creature weak, defenceless, and foolish, and he takes God to be his Provider, Preserver, Director, and, indeed, his

everything.

No man has a right to consider himself the Lord's sheep unless his nature has been renewed, for the scriptural description of unconverted men does not picture them as sheep, but as wolves or goats. A sheep is an object of property, not a wild animal; its owner sets great store by it, and frequently it is bought with a great price. It is well to know, as certainly as David did, that we belong to the Lord.

There is a noble tone of confidence about this sentence. There is no "if" nor "but," nor even "I hope so;" but he says, "The Lord *is* my shepherd." We must cultivate the spirit of assured dependence upon our heavenly Father. The sweetest word of the whole is that monosyllable, "*My*." He does not say, "The Lord is the shepherd of the world at large, and leadeth forth the multitude as his flock," but "The Lord is *my* shepherd;" if he be a Shepherd to no one else, he is a Shepherd to *me*; he cares for *me*, watches over *me*, and preserves *me*. The words are in the present tense. Whatever be the believer's position, he is even now under the pastoral care of Jehovah.

The next words are a sort of inference from the first statement — they are positive — "*I shall not want*." I might want otherwise, but when the Lord is my Shepherd he is able to supply my needs, and he is certainly willing to do so, for his heart is full of love, and therefore "*I shall not want.*" I shall not lack for *temporal things*. Does he not feed the ravens, and cause the lilies to grow? How, then, can he leave his children to starve? I shall not want *for spirituals*, I know that his grace will be sufficient for me. Resting in him he will say to me, "As thy day so shall thy strength be." I may not possess all that I wish for, but "I shall not *want*." Others, far wealthier and wiser than I, may want, but "*I shall not*." "The young lions *do* lack, and suffer hunger: but they that seek the Lord shall not want any good thing."

It is not only "I do not want," but "I *shall not* want." Come what may, if famine should devastate the land, or calamity destroy the city, *"I shall not want."* Old age with its feebleness shall not bring me any lack, and even death with its gloom shall not find me destitute. I have all things and abound; not because I have a good store of money in the bank, not because I have skill and wit with which to win my bread, but because *"The Lord is my shepherd."* The wicked always want, but the righteous never; a sinner's heart is far from satisfaction, but a gracious spirit dwells in the palace of content.

2. *"He maketh me to lie down in green pastures: he leadeth me beside the still waters."* The Christian life has two elements in it, the contemplative and the

active, and both of these are richly provided for. First, the contemplative. *"He maketh me to lie down in green pastures."*

What are these *"green pastures"* but the Scriptures of truth — always fresh, always rich, and never exhausted? There is no fear of biting the bare ground where the grass is long enough for the flock to lie down in it. Sweet and full are the doctrines of the gospel; fit food for souls, as tender grass is natural nutriment for sheep. When by faith we are enabled to find rest in the promises, we are like the sheep that lie down in the midst of the pasture; we find at the same moment both provender and peace, rest and refreshment, serenity and satisfaction.

But observe: "*He maketh* me to lie down." It is the Lord who graciously enables us to perceive the preciousness of his truth, and to feed upon it. How grateful ought we to be for the power to appropriate the promises! There are some distracted souls who would give worlds if they could but do this. They know the blessedness of it, but they cannot say that this blessedness is theirs. They know the "*green pastures*", but they are not made to "*lie down*" in them. Those believers who have for years enjoyed a "full assurance of faith" should greatly bless their gracious God.

The second part of a vigorous Christian's life consists in gracious activity. We not only think, but we act. We are not always lying down to feed, but are journeying onward toward perfection; hence we read, *"he leadeth me beside the still waters."* What are these *"still waters"* but the influences and graces of his blessed Spirit? His Spirit attends us in various operations, like waters — in the plural — to cleanse, to refresh, to fertilise, to cherish. They are *"still* waters," for the Holy Ghost loves peace, and sounds no trumpet of ostentation in his operations. He may flow into our soul, but not into our neighbour's, and therefore our neighbour may not perceive the divine presence; and though the blessed Spirit may be pouring his floods into one heart, yet he that sitteth next to the

favoured one may know no-
thing of it.

"In sacred silence of the mind
My heaven, and there my God I find."

Still waters run deep. Nothing
more noisy than an empty
drum. That silence is golden
indeed in which the Holy Spirit
meets with the souls of his
saints. Not to raging waves of
strife, but to peaceful streams
of holy love does the Spirit of
God conduct the chosen sheep.
He is a dove, not an eagle; the
dew, not the hurricane. Our
Lord leads us beside these "*still
waters*;" we could not go there
of ourselves, we need his gui-
dance, therefore it is said, "*he
leadeth me.*" He does not drive
us. Moses drives us by the law,
but Jesus leads us by his exam-

58

ple, and the gentle drawings of his love.

3. *"He restoreth my soul."* When the soul grows sorrowful he revives it; when it is sinful he sanctifies it; when it is weak he strengthens it. *"He"* does it. His ministers could not do it if he did not. His Word would not avail by itself. "He *restoreth* my soul." Are any of us low in grace? Do we feel that our spirituality is at its lowest ebb? He who turns the ebb into the flood can soon restore our soul. Pray to him, then, for the blessing — "Restore thou me, thou Shepherd of my soul."

"He leadeth me in the paths of righteousness for his name's sake." The Christian delights to be obedient, but it is the obedience of love, to which he

59

is constrained by the example of his Master. "He *leadeth* me." The Christian is not obedient to some commandments and neglectful of others; he does not pick and choose, but yields too all. Observe, that the plural is used — "the *paths* of righteousness." Whatever God may give us to do we would do it, led by his love.

Some Christians overlook the blessing of sanctification, and yet to a thoroughly renewed heart this is one of the sweetest gifts of the covenant. If we could be saved from wrath, and yet remain unregenerate, impenitent sinners, we should not be saved as we desire, for we mainly and chiefly pant to be saved *from* sin and led in the way of holiness.

All this is done out of pure free grace; "*for his name's sake.*" It is to the honour of our great Shepherd that we should be a holy people, walking in the narrow way of righteousness. If we be so led and guided we must not fail to adore our heavenly Shepherd's care.

4. "*Yea, though I walk through the valley of the shadow of death, I will fear no evil: for thou art with me; thy rod and thy staff they comfort me.*" This unspeakably delightful verse has been sung on many a dying bed, and has helped to make the dark valley bright times out of mind. Every word in it has a wealth of meaning.

"Yea, though I *walk*," as if the believer did not quicken his pace when he came to die, but still calmly *walked* with God. To walk indicates the steady advance of a soul which knows its road, knows its end, resolves to follow the path, feels quite safe, and is therefore perfectly calm and composed. The dying saint is not in a flurry, he does not run as though he were alarmed, nor stand still as though he would go no further, he is not confounded nor ashamed, and therefore keeps to his old pace. Observe that it is not walking *in* the valley, but *through* the valley. We go through the dark tunnel of death and emerge into the light of immortality. We do not die, we do but sleep to wake in glory. Death is not the house but the porch, not the goal but the passage to it. The dying article is called a *valley*. The storm breaks on the mountain, but the valley is the place of quietude, and thus full often the last days of the Christian are the most peaceful in his whole career; the mountain is bleak and bare, but the valley is rich with golden sheaves, and many a saint has reaped more joy and knowledge when he came to die than he ever knew while he lived.

And, then, it is not "the valley of death," but "the valley *of the shadow* of death," for death in its substance has been removed, and only the shadow of it remains. Some one has said that when there is a shadow there must be light somewhere, and so there is. Death stands by the side of the highway in which we have to travel, and the light of heaven shining upon him throws a shadow across our path; let us then rejoice that there is a light beyond. Nobody is afraid of a shadow, for a shadow cannot stop a man's pathway even for a moment. The shadow of a dog cannot bite; the shadow of a sword cannot kill; the shadow of death cannot destroy us. Let us not, therefore, be afraid.

"I will fear no evil." He does not say there shall not be any evil; he had got beyond even that high assurance, and knew that Jesus had put all evil away; but "I will *fear* no evil;" as if even his fears, those shadows of evil, were gone for ever. The worst evils of life are those which do not exist except in our

64

imagination. If we had no troubles but real troubles, we should not have a tenth part of our present sorrows. We feel a thousand deaths in fearing one, but the psalmist was cured of the disease of fearing. "I will fear *no evil*," not even the Evil One himself; I will not dread the last enemy, I will look upon him as a conquered foe, an enemy to be destroyed.

"*For thou art with me.*" This is the joy of the Christian! "*Thou* art with me." The little child out at sea in the storm is not frightened like all the other passengers on board the vessel, it is asleep in its mother's bosom; it is enough for it that its mother is with it; and it should be enough for the believer to know that Christ is with him.

"*Thou* art with me; I have, in having thee, all that I can crave: I have perfect comfort and absolute security, for *thou* art with me."

"*Thy rod and thy staff*," by which thou governest and rulest thy flock, the ensigns of thy sovereignty and of thy gracious care — "*they comfort me*." I will believe that thou reignest still. The rod of Jesus shall still be over me as the sovereign succour of my soul.

Many persons profess to receive much comfort from the hope that they shall not die. Certainly there will be some who will be "alive and remain" at the coming of the Lord, but is there so very much of advantage in such an escape from death as to make it the object of

Christian desire? A wise man might prefer of the two to die, for those who shall not die, but who "shall be caught up together with the Lord in the air," will be losers rather than gainers. They will lose that actual fellowship with Christ in the tomb which dying saints will have, and we are expressly told they shall have no preference beyond those who are asleep. Let us be of Paul's mind when he said that "To die is gain," and think of "departing to be with Christ, which is far better." This twenty-third psalm is not worn out, and it is as sweet in a believer's ear now as it was in David's time, let novelty hunters say what they will.

5. "*Thou preparest a table before me in the presence of mine enemies.*" The good man has his enemies. He would not be like his Lord if he had not. If we were without enemies we might fear that we were not the friends of God, for the friendship of the world is enmity to God. Yet see the quietude of the godly man in spite of, and in the sight of, his enemies. How refreshing is his calm bravery!

"*Thou preparest a table before me.*" When a soldier is in the presence of his enemies, if he eats at all he snatches a hasty meal, and away he hastens to the fight. But observe: "Thou *preparest* a table," just as a servant does when she unfolds the damask cloth and displays the ornaments of the feast on an ordinary peaceful occasion. Nothing is hurried, there is no confusion, no disturbance, the enemy is at the door, and yet God prepares a table, and the Christian sits down and eats as if everything were in perfect peace. Oh! the peace which Jehovah gives to his people, even in the midst of the most trying circumstances!

"Let earth be all in arms abroad,
They dwell in perfect peace."

"Thou anointest my head with oil." May we live in the daily enjoyment of this blessing, receiving a fresh anointing for every day's duties. Every Christian is a priest, but he cannot execute the priestly office without unction, and hence we must go day by day to God the Holy Ghost, that we may

have our heads anointed with oil. A priest without oil misses the chief qualification for this office, and the Christian priest lacks his chief fitness for service when he is devoid of new grace from on high.

"My cup runneth over." He had not only enough, a cup full, but more than enough, a cup which overflowed. A poor man may say this as well as those in higher circumstances. "What, all this, and Jesus Christ too?" said a poor cottager as she broke a piece of bread and filled a glass with cold water. Whereas a man may be ever so wealthy, but if he be discontented his cup cannot run over; it is cracked and leaks. Contentment is the philosopher's stone which turns all it touches

into gold; happy is he who has found it. Content is more than a kingdom, it is another word for happiness.

6. *"Surely goodness and mercy shall follow me all the days of my life."* This is a fact as indisputable as it is encouraging, and therefore a heavenly *verily*, or *"surely"* is set as a seal upon it. This sentence may be read, *"only* goodness and mercy,"* for there shall be unmingled mercy in our history. These twin guardian angels will aways be with me at my back and my beck. Just as when great princes go abroad they must not go unattended, so is it with the believer. Goodness and mercy follow him always — *"all the days of his life"* — the black days as well as the bright days,

71

the days of fasting as well as the days of feasting, the dreary days of winter as well as the bright days of summer. Goodness supplies our needs, and mercy blots out our sins.

"And I will dwell in the house of the Lord for ever." "A servant abideth not in the house for ever, but the son abideth ever." While I am here I will be a child at home with my God; the whole world shall be his house to me; and when I ascend into the upper chamber I shall not change my company, nor even change the house; I shall only go to dwell in the upper storey of the house of the Lord for ever.

May God grant us grace to dwell in the serene atmosphere of this most blessed Psalm!

Psalm 121

I WILL lift up mine eyes unto the hills, from whence cometh my help.

2 My help *cometh* from the LORD, which made heaven and earth.

3 He will not suffer thy foot to be moved: he that keepeth thee will not slumber.

4 Behold, he that keepeth Israel shall neither slumber nor sleep.

5 The LORD *is* thy keeper: the LORD *is* thy shade upon they right hand.

6 The sun shall not smite thee by day, nor the moon by night.

7 The LORD shall preserve

73

thee from all evil: he shall preserve thy soul.

8 The LORD shall preserve thy going out and thy coming in from this time forth, and even for evermore.

1. "*I will lift up mine eyes unto the hills, from whence cometh my help.*" It is wise to look to the strong for strength. Dwellers in the valleys are subject to many disorders for which there is no cure but a sojourn in the uplands, and it is well when they shake off their lethargy and resolve upon a climb. Down below they are the prey of marauders, and to escape from them the surest method is to fly to the strongholds upon the mountains. Often before the actual ascent the sick and plundered people looked towards the hills and longed to be upon their summits. The holy man who here sings a choice sonnet looked away from the slanderers by whom he was tormented to the

Lord who saw all from his high places, and was ready to pour down succour for his injured servant.

Help comes to saints only from above, they look elsewhere in vain: let us lift up our eyes with hope, expectancy, desire, and confidence. Satan will endeavour to keep our eyes upon our sorrows that we may be disquieted and discouraged; be it ours firmly to resolve that we will look out and look up, for there is good cheer for the eyes, and they that lift up their eyes to the eternal hills shall soon have their hearts lifted up also. The purposes of God; the divine attributes; the immutable promises; the covenant, ordered in all things and sure; the providence, predestination, and proved faithfulness of the Lord — these are the hills to which we must lift up our eyes, for from these our help must come. It is our resolve that we will not be bandaged and blindfolded, but will lift up our eyes.

Or is the text in the interrogative? Does he ask, "Shall I lift up mine eyes to the hills?" Does he feel that the highest places of the earth can afford him no shelter? Or does he renounce the idea of recruits hastening to his standard from the hardy mountaineers? and hence does he again enquire, "Whence cometh my help?" If so, the next verse answers the question, and shows whence all help must come.

2. "*My help cometh from the* LORD, *which made heaven and*

earth." What we need is help, — help powerful, efficient, constant: we need a very present help in trouble. What a mercy that we have it in our God. Our hope is in Jehovah, for our help comes from him. Help is on the road, and will not fail to reach us in due time, for he who sends it to us was never known to be too late. Jehovah who created all things is equal to every emergency; heaven and earth are at the disposal of him who made them, therefore let us be very joyful in our infinite helper. He will sooner destroy heaven and earth than permit his people to be destroyed, and the perpetual hills themselves shall bow rather than he shall fail whose ways are everlasting. We are bound

78

to look beyond heaven and earth to him who made them both: it is vain to trust the creatures: it is wise to trust the Creator.

3. *"He will not suffer thy foot to be moved."* Though the paths of life are dangerous and difficult, yet we shall stand fast, for Jehovah will not permit our feet to slide; and if he will not suffer it we shall not suffer it. If our foot will be thus kept we may be sure that our head and heart will be preserved also. In the original the words express a wish or prayer, — "May he not suffer thy foot to be moved." Promised preservation should be the subject of perpetual prayer; and we may pray believingly; for those who have God for their keeper shall be

safe from all the perils of the way. Among the hills and ravines of Palestine the literal keeping of the feet is a great mercy; but in the slippery ways of a tried and afflicted life, the boon of upholding is of priceless value, for a single false step might cause us a fall fraught with awful danger. To stand erect and pursue the even tenor of our way is a blessing which only God can give, which is worthy of the divine hand, and worthy also of perennial gratitude. Our feet shall move in progress, but they shall not be moved to their overthrow.

"He that keepeth thee will not slumber," — or "thy keeper shall not slumber." We should not stand a moment if our keeper were to sleep; we need

him by day and by night; not a single step can be safely taken except under his guardian eye. This is a choice stanza in a pilgrim song. God is the convoy and body-guard of his saints. When dangers are awake around us we are safe, for our Preserver is awake also, and will not permit us to be taken unawares. No fatigue of exhaustion can cast our God into sleep; his watchful eyes are never closed.

4. *"Behold, he that keepeth Israel shall neither slumber nor sleep."* The consoling truth must be repeated: it is too rich to be dismissed in a single line. It were well if we always imitated the sweet singer, and would dwell a little upon a choice doctrine, sucking the

honey from it. What a glorious
title is in the Hebrew — *"The
keeper of Israel,"* and how
delightful to think that no form
of unconsciousness ever steals
over him, neither the deep
slumber nor the lighter sleep.
He will never suffer the house
to be broken up by the silent
thief; he is ever on the watch,
and speedily perceives every
intruder. This is a subject of
wonder, a theme for attentive
consideration, therefore the
word *"Behold"* is set up as a
waymark. Israel fell asleep, but
his God was awake. Jacob had
neither walls, nor curtains, nor
body-guard around him; but
the Lord was in that place
though Jacob knew it not, and
therefore the defenceless man
was safe as in a castle. In after

days he mentioned God under this enchanting name — "The God that led me all my life long:" perhaps David alludes to that passage in this expression.

The word *"keepeth"* is also full of meaning: he keeps us as a rich man keeps his treasures, as a captain keeps a city with a garrison, as a royal guard keeps his monarch's head. If the former verse is in strict accuracy a prayer, this is the answer to it: it affirms the matter thus, "Lo, he shall not slumber nor sleep — the Keeper of Israel." It may also be worthy of mention that in verse three the Lord is spoken of as the personal keeper of one individual, and here of all those who are in his chosen nation, described as Israel: mercy to one saint is the

pledge of blessing to them all.
Happy are the pilgrims to
whom this psalm is a safe conduct; they may journey all the
way to the celestial city without
fear.

5. "*The Lord is thy keeper.*"
Here the preserving One, who
had been spoken of by pro-
nouns in the two previous
verses, is distinctly named —
Jehovah is thy keeper. What a
mint of meaning lies here: the
sentence is a mass of bullion,
and when coined and stamped
with the king's name it will bear
all our expenses between our
birthplace on earth and our rest
in heaven. Here is a glorious
person — *Jehovah*, assuming a
gracious office and fulfilling it
in person, — Jehovah is thy
keeper, in behalf of a favoured

individual — *thy*, and a firm assurance of revelation that it is even so at this hour — Jehovah *is* thy keeper. Can we appropriate the divine declaration? If so, we may journey onward to Jerusalem and know no fear; yea, we may journey through the valley of the shadow of death and fear no evil.

"The LORD *is thy shade upon thy right hand."* A shade gives protection from burning heat and glaring light. We cannot bear too much blessing; even divine goodness, which is a right-hand dispensation, must be toned down and shaded to suit our infirmity, and this the Lord will do for us. He will bear a shield before us, and guard the right arm with which we fight the foe. That member

which has the most of labour shall have the most of protection. When a blazing sun pours down its burning beams upon our heads the Lord Jehovah himself will interpose to shade us, and that in the most honourable manner, acting as our right-hand attendant, and placing us in comfort and safety. "The Lord at thy right hand shall smite through kings." How different this from the portion of the ungodly ones who have Satan standing at their right hand, and of those of whom Moses said, "their defence has departed from them." God is as near us as our shadow, and we are as safe as angels.

6. *"The sun shall not smite thee by day, nor the moon by*

night." None but the Lord
could shelter us from these
tremendous forces. These two
great lights rule the day and the
night, and under the lordship of
both we shall labour or rest in
equal safety. Doubtless there
are dangers of the light and of
the dark, but in both and from
both we shall be preserved —
literally from excessive heat
and from baneful chills; mysti-
cally from any injurious effects
which might follow from doctrine bright or dim; spiritually
from the evils of prosperity and
adversity; eternally from the
strain of overpowering glory
and from the pressure of terrible events, such as judgment
and the burning of the world.
Day and night make up all time:
thus the ever-present protec-

tion never ceases. All evil may be ranked as under the sun or the moon, and if neither of these can smite us we are indeed secure. God has not made a new sun or a fresh moon for his chosen, they exist under the same outward circumst-ances as others, but the power to *smite* is in their case removed from temporal agencies; saints are enriched, and not injured, by the powers which govern the earth's condition; to them has the Lord given "the precious things brought forth by the sun, and the precious things put forth by the moon," while at the same moment he has removed from them all bale and curse of heat or damp, of glare or chill.

7. "*The* LORD *shall preserve thee from all evil*," or *keep* thee

from all evil. It is a great pity
that our admirable translation
did not keep to the word *keep*
all through the psalm, for all
along it is one. God not only
keeps his own in all evil times
but from all evil influences and
operations, yea, from evils
themselves. This is a far-
reaching word of covering: it
includes everything and exclu-
des nothing: the wings of Jehovah amply guard his own from
evils great and small, tempor-
ary and eternal. There is a most
delightful double personality in
this verse: Jehovah keeps the
believer, not by agents, but by
himself; and the person pro-
tected is definitely pointed out
by the word *thee*, — it is not our
estate or name which is
shielded, but the proper perso-

nal man.

To make this even more intensely real and personal another sentence is added, *"The* LORD *shall preserve thee from all evil: he shall preserve thy soul,"* — or Jehovah will keep thy soul. Soul-keeping is the soul of keeping. If the soul be kept all is kept. The preservation of the greater includes that of the less so far as it is essential to the main design: the kernel shall be preserved, and in order thereto the shell shall be preserved also. God is the sole keeper of the soul. Our soul is kept from the dominion of sin, the infection of error, the crush of despondency, the puffing up of pride; kept from the world, the flesh, and the devil; kept for holier and greater things; kept in the love of God; kept unto the eternal kingdom and glory. What can harm a soul that is kept of the Lord?

8. "*The* LORD *shall preserve thy going out and thy coming in from this time forth, and even for evermore.*" When we go out in the morning to labour, and come home at eventide to rest, Jehovah shall keep us. When we go out in youth to begin life, and come in at the end to die, we shall experience the same keeping. Our exits and our entrances are under one protection. Three times have we the phrase, "Jehovah shall keep," as if the sacred Trinity thus sealed the word to make it sure: ought not all our fears to be slain by such a threefold flight of arrows? What anxiety can

survive this triple promise? This keeping is eternal; continuing from this time forth, even for evermore. The whole church is thus assured of everlasting security: the final perseverance of the saints is thus ensured, and the glorious immortality of believers is guaranteed. Under the ægis of such a promise we may go on pilgrimage without trembling, and venture into battle without dread. None are so safe as those whom God keeps; none so much in danger as the selfsecure. To goings out and comings in belong peculiar dangers, since every change of position turns a fresh quarter to the foe, and it is for these weak points that an especial security is provided: Jehovah will keep the door when it opens and closes, and this he will perseveringly continue to do so long as there is left a single man that trusteth in him, as long as a danger survives, and, in fact, as long as time endures. Glory be unto the Keeper of Israel, who is endeared to us under that title, since our growing sense of weakness makes us feel more deeply than ever our need of being kept. Over the reader we would breathe a benediction, couched in the verse of Keble.

"God keep thee safe from harm and sin,
Thy spirit keep; the Lord watch o'er
Thy going out, thy coming in,
From this time, evermore."

Vintage Series

Books in large print for the elderly and those with visual handicaps.

Selections from well-known authors to encourage believers today.

Authors include C.H. Spurgeon, F.B. Meyer, George Muller, J.C. Ryle, Matthew Henry.

**Daily Readings
from
Christian Focus Publications**

Each has thirty-one readings
in large print.

1. Gems from Genesis - Barbara Honour

2. Promises of Hope - Barbara Honour
   (each based on a verse from the Psalms)

3. Walking in the Way - John Tallach
   (devotional thoughts with application)

Assurance

J.C. Ryle
(in large print)

Assurance is scriptural

Assurance is desirable

Assurance is necessary for our comfort

Yet what is assurance?

Bishop Ryle examines the issue, explains clearly how to have it and encourage us to expect assurance.

100pp   *pocket paperback*